AEIPATHY

FEEL TO HEAL

ANUSTHA PAL

ISBN 979-888591003-3

This book is dedicated to my all well-wisher, who supported me for this book, to express my poetry words. I am greatly thankful to all, who is a very friendly way helped me out, to make this book successful. Great dedication to me also, who done all that, with my full honesty, grace, and patience. Even after facing taunts and discouraging emotions from a lot of people, even in an engineering long schedule finding out love for writing, to be passionate, to be humble.

thank you...

Contents

Foreword   *vii*

Preface   *ix*

  1. Vigilant   1

  2. Pastel Colors   3

  3. Neon Girl   5

  4. Old Chapter   7

  5. Blank   9

  6. Reasonless   12

  7. Fake Rituals   14

  8. Break   16

  9. Stone   18

10. Tasty   22

11. Rumors   24

12. New Home   26

13. Game Over   27

14. Goodbye To Goodbye   29

15. It's Okay To Be Not Okay   31

16. Fugue   32

17. Block   34

18. Neo   35

19. Remedy   38

20. Human Robot   40

21. Human Robot   41

22. Boundless   42

23. Mother   44

24. My Addiction   45

Contents

25. Adolescence   47

26. Bitch   48

27. Life Art   50

28. Leafy Blossom   52

29. Life Inside A Life   54

30. Scars   57

31. Chapter 31   59

32. Earphone   60

33. Desert   61

Foreword

Author of this book Ms. Anustha Pal, started her work when she was 19. she took her graduation in Bachelor of technology in computer Science and Engineering, that is too Far from writing but she knew and define her writings and poetry in that time that make her publish her thoughts and vision in the form of poetry book.

Her parents and people around her inspire her to write what she feels. She inspires people around her from being a beautiful Poet. she wrote amazing books - Scars, Door to my Soul, and Anustha diary that are too intresting to Read.

Preface

I am Anustha Pal, Now I have completed seventh semester of B. Tech and my journey take me to this book. This book is soul and I tell everything according to what I feel in few days passed and I hope all the readers enjoy my book. This book contains amazing experiences and story-based poetry that make you feel delight, with rhythm I make these poems sound good to your heart.

Thank you so much for reading!!

Author: ANUSTHA PAL

1. VIGILANT

Quoting every benchmark, never
Let my soul down
Giving rise to impatience is the heftiest
Delight ever.

I make people die to make every entity safe
For this mansion, I work hard and
Stay Vigilant.

I retrace my intentions and kept,
All the soul in the goblet of words.

The part that you never own,
Introspection lives in me.
I put ash into the quarters,
To make me clap on my lifeless ends.

Sipping, puking, plunging
clasping every dust in my lakeside
Farm,
I kill all the notion which you
heap inside your eyes.
By slaying the law of attraction
Communicating a world of hate and

AEIPATHY

Drenching past.

Your greedy eyes tumble on my body
I rugged horribly in my world.
You making me a piece of attraction
And shop me, put me like a slave.

Taking your wise thread
I stitch my life from lifeless Fabric into a beautiful frilled frock.

2. PASTEL COLORS

Pastel color found in heart sensitive
and Sensitivity is something people
Find hard to adore,
It's worthless childish but still, I own.
Awkward leg, lethal tie
Holding the harmonious world
In my one eye.

The perimeters of life are
intense and scraping
measuring length and breadth,
with scissors and knives.

Sweetness is shoddy,
bartering Like a cheap cloths
with no Standard and ignoring,
it's beauty for a piece
I try to own, but people
Make me feel dismissed.

I want to give gash
To some unknown entities,
Repository of your skills
Is truly empty, you are done.

Taking and using my recipe
To cook,
You make my taste bud experience,
something undesirable, when you cook.
Brainy storms took my head
Feeling drying like a piece of fabric on
The window side.
don't deal drastic dramatic with their head
colors pastel vanish, try to understand
Sensitivity needs sensitivity
To grow and praise.

3. NEON GIRL

The neon girl not puffed with her emotion,
her weight is ten. like a periodic table ,
she also have exception,
lived In a cottage of hundred and eight member
with their properties .
she never admit she has a big family.
people saw only lanky body
with their narrow eyes
But her noble behaviour
make people happy.
one day People's eyes
The angle of attitude might
Make you feel jealous,
she love helium , when he
fly with balloon,
Drifting with storms
To make castle in the sky
She don't desire for a
Perfect life.
odourless , colourless, mono atomic
with low chemical activity, neon have friends argon , krypton, xenon
radon occurring naturally.
one side member of family are acidic
one sided are basic, there few are neutral , that makes a family.

up to down in cottage and from left different people live with different
properties, which are ascending and descending.

Thumping her gesture
Into someone's eye
Wearing clothes in a order
You never like it.
Still a neon girl is wonderful
Part of someone's life.
living diagonally with HCl and parallel with HF side, she lights up very
quickly and glows red, her weight is light, she is inert
and her colour glows every time.

4. OLD CHAPTER

Some bitter truth,
Driving dreams in the humanity tribe
Rotating wheels tell,
How circular is our life?
Diamond crystal demons dark
Sky fell in a moment of eye
Let's end this part and start again
Without any dark side.
A lot of strings are broken
In the greed of fame and money,
Being non-judgemental
Is difficult like maths sum
To unravel,

Doors stand holding
Keys,
Difficult panicked puzzle
Riddle tells me I am foolish
People thought I my rolling eyes,
Make stories for sympathetic vibes,
But eyes sometimes, see the shattered
The part that nobody can't handle alone,
In their big brain for many years,
holding legs in the tides,

AEIPATHY

quarreling for blotches
Is an unexplainable part,
Making grievance like that
Make me a timid whiz star,
But my life is so far
people creating a suffocating world
no oxygen so far.
Now we need an eye on
old chapter to restart.

5. BLANK

Some part of life is hard
Is worthy

Unclean and dirty,
Mystery irreversible, end
Blow cigar of life.

Bitter world and true thoughts are
Deeply hurting my pure vibes.

Aftermaths of being so
Unworthy, let me feel tired

Dreaming something is like
Residing two days in my favorite apparel.

Cluster raining drops of summary,
June is a month that hates January.

scorn the season of rain
It's s true cold in January something
About my sphere and my cold soul.

Jumble words keep making

AEIPATHY

My dictionary fly,

Conducting a judgments
out of mind.

Clumsy legs don't walk
Too
Long with the dress that flickers and
With pencil heels

It is not easy and not
Available for long like a train,

Keep the rhythm and eye your desire
And on your mind though,

Are you ill?
Is also a part of art.

Falling for ice cream,
Begging for more chocolate
To my mom.

Dumb mind-set forgot about
The beauty and affection

Getting truly Lumbering and
Grinning in my mind

Trauma is hitting me hard
I think I am dying for some parts.

6. REASONLESS

Eyes are inflating to capture
a Blind smile,
Catching your bottle of perfume and
took your fragrance in my life,
control my drift to stop my agony
again and again, opening my lights,
to close the shattered parts.
I am not a nicely defined mule,
But I am able to eradicate your
Every dream.
I love the long mountains and lap
of nature, who understood my choices
and enhancement.

Your tongue is felting, you are
Tasteless.
Like your communication skills
Behave like a maniac.
Your wood turn into ashes,
You put your mind into a hearth.

Reaching windfall,
Is just the momentum of time.

looking at every reason,
why you break others, for a diamond mine
try to become amazing warm light,
but Eyebrow twist, turn and tell
that you are a mess running
Around.

Screaming in my porch is
Just a phony
But dear my soul is deaf,
I can't hear cacophonies,
neglected every manipulation.

You perpetrated enough,
This is not the end.
because some stories have no connections.

7. FAKE RITUALS

The day I stop
Seeking my lunatic behaviour,
Is the end of my carelessness.

For not letting down others,
Living in the adobe of the dead.
Hiding my own cravings and dreams,
Just walking in narrow lanes
to save Rituals having no meaning
in today's world.

Why I stopped festooning me,
My expensive experience ends?
But what about my own perceptions
that we live only once.
A cloth you can't wear?
to become particle of goddess,
still drink whole ocean,
for people thoughts and opinions we own
to adjust.

Yes Belle are found sweet to
Talk But my ridiculous seasonings
describe only the terrible ends.

disturbing Your crystal parts,
Sorry for a long list of disapproval
It is not easy to regret about what you just lost,
I am just trying stride to play
with life and it's wind captivating my smile.
after everything I start believing in me and
start working for my character and what makes
my smile.

8. BREAK

I try to forget the backdoor window, Where every night, My eyes stare at
someone,
In the moonlight,
My door lets people enter into my Soul.

My shady plot holds its own rainbow,
Which always shimmer and melodious because
Of beautiful wind chime,
I raise my eyebrows, for reaching my heart.

When I probably about to End,
people mixed words and
Reply,
Into a piece of garlic I can't bite.
I just Love Lustre of the sun that come every morning ,
at my window.
Because they add Mascara To my
Eyes.

My bread butter life i
become a fantasy of fairy-tale
Living in scars let me tell
how it feels, when you haven't find the ,

one who is right
But this is what I am
Felting from long ,

That it's better that I take,
A Break .
Instead of holding my kite
in the wind , which evacuate me far,
because I have no stamina to surprise people.
Door to my soul i have closed to give me a break
from the city and swore
Sometimes breaks give ideas what next needs to explore.

9. STONE

We are the stones, or we aren't?
Someone who feels,
and supposed to express.
Feelings are the expression
you solve every day.
a new equation on my way
Twinkling is a moment that shimmer, to
you are touching the star without moving
so far,
you don't get their physically but your
vision just touches the highest tree.
Gloomy glossy sky taught me,
About the patience that
I rust, to hold in my
Smile.
But stone like me you never found.
I don't even smile when I don't like it.
Stone has some qualities,
that I also hold.
To be brave and courageous is
Is my life goal.
Stop being lazy, love to be
A wild dandelion or daisy.
Stop being guilty, surprisingly

I glad on that chunks of thoughts,
that I brought.
I clasping the peace like I am a pebble
In grass.

But the life utterance hold me
Like the breeze, reading ocean high tides
like a summery,
And the wave take salt and water
away and mix them anyway.

One day sea crying in hurricanes
I just go to fill cracks of her walls,
How small of me I guess but,
this is not what I am all about.

An ocean inside me tell me that
We are at an equilibrium equation with
Different constants of me and the sea.

But mathematics hold the
Magic of numbers,
But I am falling like a broken
twig.

Somehow I have just fallen in that
Well,
And can never come up like

AEIPATHY

It is my ritual place.

So I started calling to make
Someone fool!!!
A small boy with numb
Innocent smiles and true talking.

I make him a broker to get
What I want.
By asking for serenity, I
crosses my boundaries.

Innocence is something
That don't find odds,
And the hand of friendship
I took out of well,
make others fool,
to our rituals and rules.
Magic of maths and calculus
Integrate my passions for a remote craft.
Now, I leave him in the spring
because I am out of a prison
now I am in different vision
This is virtue of freedom ,
And existing bodies may live or
Die.
openness don't need to weapon
to fight.

My sensitivities are at their loftiest
Ratio .
Become immortal and don't bend
I am a stone until this world will end.

10. TASTY

Sweet and sour fruits on tree,
Everything else remaining is bitter like
Wine and Whisky,
Salty n spicy is something I love most
But salty fruits are not found on any tree?
Salt only found in rocks and sea
and ocean eyes,

.

tears hold salt with emotion's kite.
which give the energy to fight,
that know how to survive, even
failures felt like our world disappears
but eyes remove the anxiety and
make you fly.
theory of everything say,
eyes are connected to the ocean
that's why eye and sea contain
salt in their water
I just don't know why?
sweet chocolate, sour tamarind
bitter medicine and bitter else everything
bitter is the flavour of taunt
bitter is language enemy speak,
bitter is the day ,which don't end well

bitter are the failures , you not let you
in peace.
bitter are the feelings , which are broken
even when you judge.
sweetness found in the friend's talk
sometimes when you hug your mom,
sometimes by getting flowers from the
lover, even if nothing is there.

salt found in some salty boys,
who shout when not feel fun,
but in taste salt make everything
tasty like rolls,
spicy eatable combine with salt,
and gives us tasty food,
some people say it junk food , which
is not healthy
but tasting it after once, our tongue
just admit, if it is consume in limit
it will give you the best taste.

11. RUMORS

Have you heard about the rumours?
The biggest rumour in today's world is
Being tall?
Being afraid of smiling?
A child starting his life at 12?
Do you know?
Rumours say
Fancy cloth broke the
Heart of men,
A toy car hit the laptop
While jeans are a passion to
Follow,
Dreams are onion smiles,
Liking has broken
The cup of tea,
Poppy is colour to
Paint on your wall,
I eat the doors and window
There is too much light, so I open
The torch.
Man buy a wooden cardboard
To gift to niece,
She wear the toothbrush on
Her wedding,

I m worried that I passed in each
Subject
Meeta and David are hell depress
They are topper this year,
Buttons look nice on her cheeks
This is a poetry not a song so
What should I need to off to
Tell you that ,It is the end.

12. NEW HOME

Start loving being empty
Now I am on the edge of infinity.
Realising l am not enough for anybody,
but Dark twilights can't took my glory
Weekends nights are unusual,
Doom, Deadline is arrived
My expectations are not so high
I am comfortable with my own sky.
The reason pail vision leaking My thoughts,
I am Trying to collect it,
drop by drop.

Still every moment is falling,
Trying to put sunglasses on My eyes,
So that I can make people confuse about my bly .
Life is clean still smudged like My laundry,
every minute detail Into a piece of overthinking ,
After me , this body die but these poems tell
story of a twenty one old year girl with a smile .

13. GAME OVER

I am just playing a game
In which, my victory is impossible
Through some unsatisfied soul,
And eyes I revert the whole sky.

Dreams of glimpse are at my porch,
I have some stories left unlearned
Some wishes are hidden in the mighty eye,
Some panic attacks are in my
Heart,
Its helfy stars don't like my sky

Catching the fireballs in my
Head
Draining all the knowledge of
Mine into your life

Sometimes your achievement
Become my awards,
Losing or winning doesn't perfect
Asset for life,
Wine kind of substance is
pell-mell into my mind.

You can afford a celebration
Just through a wine ,
Be divine of your life
So that you can took yourself
In both celebration and scars.

14. GOODBYE TO GOODBYE

Take my all shimmery ornaments,
Gift me a blank night,
I Keep aspiring,
about remembrance and old time.
When my glowing golden gist
make me carless,
when people notify, that you are just
part of the journey, not a terminal
of their dream.
I used to know people better,
by this concept of time.

When I glanced upon the photograph,
you kept in your wallet all the time,
My clouds are disappearing,
but my sunshine holds hope in my eyes.

Sipping all that venom,
Like I am in python of someone's life,
Bite bitter feelings like it's my
Crazy maniac addiction to hold,

fragmented pieces in my mind.

I keep watching my brook
Flowing non-stop,
Just don't keep wishing
More and more, cause I am
not a shop.
your grocery store,
Everything remains in the draft box,
I write an email to my bitch inky character,
I take my flight,
Saying my memories,
hey and bye to life,
And Say GOODBYE TO GOODBYE.

15. IT'S OKAY TO BE NOT OKAY

Creating a good conscience Harsh and kind, only aphorism works, no other procedure works Tongue if speak in hurry And inline, Leaving spoken words Out of timeline.

Your pain is working too Fine, I just decline Your sobriety tell about Your strict schedule and time.

Conditionality is a factor Affecting me as a version get degraded, Some uneasy decisions bound Me to regret,

I wonder why my calculations are failed? Like Prescription that doctor Never gives up.

I bought medicine for my Bypass heart Fatigue inside tell about my Blind eyes, Being ok and smiling work Right,

Life is meaningless, And tell you're hear, It's okay to be not okay.

16. FUGUE

Amnesia lying in my veins,
With a comforter, I am staying in
My bed,

I draw a portrait of night, to get asleep
After a long run of memories

Closed window casement of my room is
rusting, because of being closed for years
Hiding into my curtains.

winding Maze which ruins
All-day,
Let my pace freeze and
Leave me this way

I barely open the drape
To touch my life
Because infinity lies
Limits subtracting vision of pardon eyes.
Living in the cold inky black careless world, Like my personality bly.

But that curse kept
Me awake,

My amnesia makes me
Different from character
Either way.

Feeling is a journey
Never halt,
It is the sign that you are
Alive.

17. BLOCK

I am a block, living in a block
Some people block, to block all the Uncertainty,

So I make my feelings blocked,
I block me to block all that issues,
That makes me live in a black blocked box.

I dive deeper to reach a block
Where nobody is blocked, but my
Books and subjects tell you cannot draw
A flowchart and a vigorous life without coming out of insecurities block.

I pursue a wooden block to teach,
My mind about the clock,
Under a Wooden block holding anxiety in a stock,
in the deep woods a creature whose wings block In a spider web
she doesn't have Jeb so she searches on the web

how to Unblock others and own feelings, That l lock
God says you have to be courageous
stop living in a cowardly block
And unblock your wings and flaws and one day all that feeling
That you put in an anxiety block stops.

18. NEO

Trees are not wobbling and
stay on their Place for long,
In this pandemic, they hold Their branches
and come out Of soil withholding their
Packet of water and soil in polythene.

neo is my Margosa tree,
neo like my family,
in summer he gave me shade,
in winter give his branches for the fire.
now he turns forty this year,
he standing in his place and being
loyal from so long,
he gives space to birds and squirrel
to chirp on,
squirrel used to shout at my dog
She has loved Neo for so long.

neo loves to fall his leaves on me,
when it's spring,
He took care of the air that I am breathing in.
neo always help other
give a home to others, but for the sake of help
a parasite growing with his help,

AEIPATHY

she takes her nutrition, her name is
money plant, but he loves her like
a guy loves his girl,
he knows she is a parasite but still
he helps,
good things grow, like symbiotic
relationship of neo,
he falls, he grow, having his
fruits he gave me,
but they are bitter so I can't
take them although.
but neo make green,
and he is keen,
Saying to me it's an awful
Thing, but like all humans, Neo also needs food.

Running in a rush, through Roots.
Influencing me that in this Cold They also
I need a sweater of wool.

I go into their market
And buy a closed sweater for him,
After wearing that,
he asked How I thank You for This feat.

I replied very politely your
Oxygen is enough
No need for thanks and

all we need is you live in your peace,

He broke a branch and say to me
I will be your best friend and I save
you from invisible enemies.
and neo sat with.

19. REMEDY

Taking the whole forbearance
In my birds chirping every day,
To take me in the remote
After pouring infinite fractions
Of my heart On my decision,
The whole of me yet to come.

The issues of the brain
Mend my soul, block the trauma.
Small talk becomes my strength.
boundaries do not own
My intention,
Taking my breath to far from earth
To sky ,
I feel dandelion flower on my coffin
Doom of my thoughts pulling
My imagination to leave the cage of
Anxiety.

I getting to break my lofty voice
To a pretty lady
Expenses showing me all the
Smoothness capital can afford,
But I used to memorize the day

When snake bites and venom
In my nerve took all in me
And everything I ever have.
So I become loin within my
Own voice and crush that window
Panel to help me to cure my wounds,
To get out of venom
And make me tough like walking
In the strain.

20. HUMAN ROBOT

The wires of feelings
Make us a robot ,
One wrong connection, makes Loss self esteem
One right drift shake your
Eyes to the person you are waiting for.
Fairy tale journey start with
A lover who stayed,
When socket of emotion break , robot is about to dead
Break Out pain ,
it is just like the current
Of 440 volts is it?
It fail other definition and functionalities, to recover wiring,
arduino Start their work,
Make humanity unique robots, being Careless make you human pull out
your wiring and be alive,
AEIPATHY
be human.

21. HUMAN ROBOT

The wires of feelings
Make us a robot,
One wrong connection makes
Loss self-esteem
One right drift shake your
Eyes to the person you are waiting for.

Fairy tale journey starts with
A lover who stayed,
When the socket of emotion breaks,
robot is about to dead
Break Out pain,
it is just like the current
Of 440 volts is it?

It fail other definition and functionalities,
to recover wiring,
arduino Start their work,
Make humanity unique robots,
being Careless make you human
pull out your wiring and be alive,
be human.

22. BOUNDLESS

My isolated kindness want a
Listener to heed.

All you need is my agony
All my hopes are breaking down.
I am getting a huge bag and
a blunt inky sky to make frills,
like my grandma.

Nobody pretend I am virtuous,
I felt like I am pebble across a sea,
Gawking thunder and hurricane
aloof alone features of life don't need
even a caption for it.
My uncrowned anecdotes.

All my Life, lies in my bucket,
Everybody come and
take my Glitter now only
Things lefts are flies,
my ancillary butterflies,
I have to love them foe what
they are.
Chameleon owned every

colour but yes,
My daisy blur listener,
you all live in a world of high
time, storms can't make you die.
you live in a big technocrat time
be different, difficult to be your own kind.

23. MOTHER

Life is dictionary
Part of life is a book
Book is a mixture word
Words are a mixture of the alphabet.
Alphabet come from sound
Sound comes from throat
Throat comes to the body.
Body comes from a
Mother,
Mother comes from another
Mother,
Another mother comes from
Another mother.
This is how our life ends
On mother
With grace, pace and full
Respect mother is a creator
of everything and every phase.

24. MY ADDICTION

It is strange that I
Lost all my addiction,
Life need everything back,
But my symptoms tell that
I glint without anything.
Walking on the porch, a place of
Battle and scars,
Know that I own one smile.
In a life full of presumptions and witches,
Take my every part
My addiction leaves my heart Infraction,

The friction of my shoes
The wink in my eyes
Trick all my life
Took all my sincerity into my addiction.
My addiction holding the mountains,
holding pages of life in a sequence,
Unless I uphold the dirt and space bar.
It's assumptions that build our life so far,
still, people hate addiction,
which work maniac and turn,
into gold your breathless life.
Addiction is the madness,

I saw it, in my dreams.
I use to dream so,
l wake up from my sleep.
Everything that hurts does not need space.
Your mind is enough to live in an addiction of grace.

25. ADOLESCENCE

Up in the star, in the world of
Moon n star
Custom and traditional wear unclean
Lenses,
Self-esteem humiliated by peer attempts,
Confused crazy drive,
Adolescents holding dreams on fire
Strumming patterns make rhythm attractive
Being inoffensive situation
Hurting me this time,
Closed life also holding
some unclosed Doors.
Being not able to enjoy some
basic sound
And loud roaring at your door
To be fearlessly out this time,
The length of breath is typical
To notice,
How much time it take to overcome
From a realization, it is hard to make it.
Adolescence swallow childhood but
Gives dreams big.

26. BITCH

When bitch inside me cry
I feel the ocean in my eyes ,
it is like hurting and paining
My lovely eyes .

Scorching sun touching
My breath like a corner
Never reached

Full of emptiness and
Blindness my rings are destroying.

I can handle the cracks
But can't handle these bitch vibes.

Damned dirty shores uneasy unproved,
Holding my every on shore, took
umbrella into my hand to protect my soul.

My future is dying and
Hearing my heart just
Want nothing,

Far from infinity my

Patience die,
I see bitch inside me
Juggling, just want to
Run to the sky
Say one day I also
Die .

I see atmosphere all around
That was not really kind
My honesty living for years
In pitch dirty n blind

I spend hazy night to watch
The infinity of lies
Because of something crazy
Inside me ,
My bitch is still alive .

27. LIFE ART

You know it is complicated
To be What you are.
Daily facts make you
Shaky.
Sharing makes you blunt.
And give you tears for fears
For what you pleaded since
Last year.
hunting for sky
Having no way to escape.
Just small talk to communicate.

Your drawback is my secret,
I can't share with this earth.
To blackmail you through your
ill arts is not my skill.
Throw your soft parts,
This is what you are sneaking all apart.
Making distance give intimacy
You don't want to lose,
We are unable to skip,
This is the meal of the life wheel.
Body has some purity
And puffed emotions.

That you desire to hire
But eventually knowing
Everything is awful and ugly.
You carry your intuition
Into the bars .
Into the bottle of wine to
Fulfil your heart.
Wearing shiny blotches,
You decorated up your deformity,
But having shine to hide.
Some technocrat with their
shocking tails
Make you unaware of blogs
You watch too long.
Life Skill is a craft to
Learn more about life
Stitches that make you
Mastermind.

28. LEAFY BLOSSOM

Isolation is an island,
I want to reach
reading someone's aura
I want to teach
I am wearing the gemstones,
Which entire change my point of view to
what you want to be.
I get up to know,
What's great here!!
because distinct identity purchased
same entity.
But after a day, there is
No way to escape these
tedious eyes.
Geometry of face
create the blunder in knowing
inner beauty and persona
of that face.
stagecraft take the glory of reality,
Holding in their heart, what went wrong.
Some dry flowers, attached
The branch burdens them.
Some fragile moment and cure
Take hands into hands.

Now loving me is like,
Loving what I have.
In order to be a curious
Askhole,
I want to ask about my journey
What you think about my life
And emotions?
Do you want to hold me?
Even if I have water in my eyes?
At the moment people blame me
That I steal their dog?
I go for a walk with solitary
Or when I kick my stones for fun?
What do you love in me?
My future advice?
Or the music I listen
Or even if you know
Broken things hurt,
It's like I am broken
In your hand?
Your courage to bleed to
Hold my pieces
All excuses are over
And we have always on a
New trip
To explore to be the best one.

29. LIFE INSIDE A LIFE

We Daily brush-up and daily die
up and downs are part of life
I never thought I can also be
a chameleon in real-time.

Castle of magnificence and
grandeur, I put in a suitcase fastened
and aloof Alone,

I never know that when you
Unpack or interrogate through your soul,
You are waiting for some serenity
To explore humble compassion.

Sprinkle drizzle in your Eyes,
Wear a fragrance that smells shy,
Become a hostage of life
And reach the blind world
and perished basic qualities.

blue Curtains and brown doors,
Even silver locks and green keys try

To preach,
about my selfless qualities.

I am deaf but my words
speak.
Curled lashes and scarlet
lips tricked,
Wearing honesty on my face
And make me queen
but living in a cage.

A virtual word full of mercy
full of snakes,
can't match my imagination
in that way,
Parallel thoughts and jiggling
polished notion trying to escape.

Hollow void bellflowers
attracting me,
through their fragrance.
Where my eyes are staring
And walking through,

It's like life is inside a poster
Of movie and I am a villain
Like I am an actress with the
dark past

But with the end of the day
I found myself in a satchel
Locked with emotions
And worldliness
But I know still, I am polite
and kind.
this is how we use
to live two personalities at once,
one which we show and one which we hide
this is how life inside a life.

30. SCARS

*Darting portrayals
of respect betrayal ,
Staying in moments
and craft of words
working on me.*

*I vanish in the appearance
of my face,
I dissolve me like
I am lying in a salt lake .
Assuming incidents and
scars they take me
Too far ,*

*Away from the dilemma,
Away from my past
I make a Small home,
l am deeply owner
Of this home.*

*Living in a red brick house
look like a monastery ,
Fluid form of emotion*

AEIPATHY

vaporizing my tears,
It swings flirty and foggy.

Cumulonimbus rumbling in
my small sky,
where l am at my end asking
For some letters I wrote.
You forget to reward me.
For being a good example of folks,
And the house of million thrones.

When I open my eyes,
l am inside a doom
Handing my pillow and numbness,
I take deep last breath and
just reach heaven.

Chapter31

32. EARPHONE

Someone unknown, who knows
My every zone are my earphones
Listening to my feeling the entire day
and not getting bored,
Holding my merry and
Emotions with no fear
fork my life with
shimmery gleaming thoughts,
Earphones just read my sound notes,
For several times.
sometimes I hold no love, no memory
No ashes to ground my justice,
earphone help me to stay in a melody
for that random moments to hear
it collects Pieces of sound to make
I feel safe, these help to avoid
noise from space.
But they also let to touch the
voices from people are near us.
they are clones, they are part of the phone
they know your limitations and sky
and help you define.

33. DESERT

Camel on the desert who is old,
Sand that is hot and cold,
In different timings, a waterless place
A land of dark nights, their sand store
secret survival arts.

Jumping to catch the emotion
Turn in a lifelong mirage I can't
Even find,

A key of mind is pushed on my
Neck, that open door of my mind
thirsty soul believes in ghoul,

These mirrors confused between
What is real or what is part of
Stress,

I can't go with dumping and burying
My thoughts, this land is lifeless,

Desert has no water to make you
Feel delighted,
Jellyfish can't make their home

AEIPATHY

In a decent mirage right?

Same way I can't address me
In the world of data lake,

Turning wires , stacking emotions
dry the desert creatures emotion

My word of art embarrassed by
Making the saddest closet.

Geometry of works don't make
Go degree right.

Letters still dumped on posted Every time,
They are like cactus, in people 's eye.

My polished nail are dead, they
Don't believe in nail colours all the Time,
some dead bodies painted in the desert,
The chemical works so fine.

Catching and dropping emotions
And tired eyes,

I stuck on a mind game
Like this desert mirage in my mind.

ANUSTHA PAL

A Land lost greenery in time,
our mind are desert with technocrat
arts that's what I find in the desert of mind.

Thank you so much for reading this book...